To: Hannah Belle
  + Libbey Lu
Love: Mama

Mothers' Day
2000

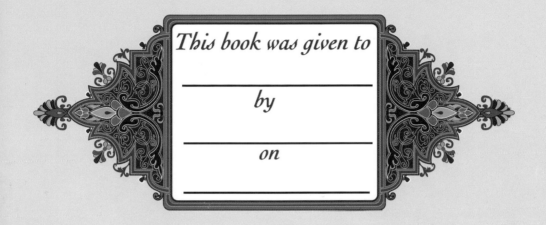

This book was given to

_____

by

_____

on

_____

# A Child's Garden of Virtues

## Stories About Virtues

*Compiled by Peg Augustine*
*Illustrated by Teresa Harper*

**DIMENSIONS**
**FOR LIVING**
NASHVILLE

# Contents

# A Child's Garden of
# VIRTUES

 # aith

When we say we have faith in something, we mean that we believe it with our whole hearts. We have faith in God and in God's son, Jesus. We trust God and Jesus and we will be loyal to them, no matter what happens. We believe that God and Jesus will be loyal to us, too. They will help us through bad times and be happy with us during good times.

# A LITTLE GIRL WHO HELPED

*II Kings 5:1-4, 9-14; Ephesians 4:32*

A LITTLE girl lived in the home of a kind man named Naaman. It was a beautiful house and there were many helpers. The little girl was one of the helpers who did many things for Naaman's wife. Even though it was a beautiful home, no one was happy. Naaman was very sick. None of the doctors had been able to make him well.

One day the little girl was helping her mistress, Naaman's wife. She sat winding red yarn into a ball while her mistress sewed. The little girl said, "It makes me sad that Naaman is sick. I wish he might go to see a good helper in the land where I used to live. The helper is Elisha. He has helped many people and I think he might make Naaman well."

How happy the mistress was to hear about Elisha. "We must tell Naaman at once," she said. Quickly the mistress sent a servant to tell Naaman about Elisha.

When Naaman heard the good news, he said, "I will go at once to see this man, Elisha." Everyone helped to get Naaman ready. Then he and his servants drove away in a chariot.

"It will take a long time for Naaman to get to Elisha's house," said the little girl. "I am sure God will help Elisha make Naaman well again."

After many days, Naaman returned. Everyone ran out to meet him. He stepped from the chariot. His face was happy. His eyes were shining. His voice was strong. "I am well, I am well," he called as he ran to the house.

Naaman came to where the little girl was standing. "Thank you for telling me about Elisha, the man of God. He told me to go wash in the river Jordan. I went and did as Elisha told me. I am well."

The little girl was glad that she had been able to help these people who had been kind to her.

# A LITTLE SEED

*Mark 4:31-32*

THERE was once a little seed. It was so tiny that when a woman held it in her hand she could hardly see it.

"This is a mustard seed," said the good woman. "I will plant it in my garden. Mustard will taste good with my dinner."

So the woman dug up the earth to make a soft bed for the tiny seed. She dropped the tiny seed in the earth and covered it. No one could see it. No one could find it.

But the sun shone on the earth where the tiny seed lay. Some days raindrops fell on the earth where the tiny seed lay. When there was no rain the good woman sprinkled water on the earth where the tiny seed lay.

By and by a tiny green stalk came up where the tiny seed lay. By and by some tiny green leaves came out on the tiny green stalk. "My mustard plant!" said the good woman. And she softened the earth around it. She sprinkled water on it.

Sun shone on the mustard plant. Rain fell on the mustard plant. It grew and grew. It grew tall. It spread out branches with green leaves on them. "My mustard plant is taller than I am," said the good woman.

One day two birds flew up into the mustard plant. "See! See! See!" called the father bird. "What a fine place for a nest!" "Whee, Whee!" answered the mother bird. "A cozy home among these leaves!"

The nest was built. And not long after there were baby birds

in that nest. When it was hot the leaves of the tall mustard plant shaded the baby birds from the sun. When the rain fell the leaves of the tall mustard plant kept the baby birds dry and warm.

One day Jesus came along with his friends. He saw the tall mustard plant. He heard the baby birds chirping in their nest. He remembered how tiny a little mustard seed is. And he told the story I have just told you.

# THE IMPATIENT FARMER

A FARMER walked by the side of his cornfields in the springtime. A frown was on his face, for there had been no rain for several weeks, and the earth was hard from the dry winds blowing from the east. The young corn had not been able to spring up.

As he looked over the long ridges that stretched in rows before him, he began to grumble and say:

"The harvest will be late, and everything will go wrong."

He frowned more and more, and complained against the sky because there was no rain; against the earth because it was so dry; against the corn because it had not sprung up. Going to his comfortable home, he complained to his wife that the drought would ruin the harvest.

His wife, however, spoke cheerful words, and, taking her Bible, she wrote some words from God on the very first page and, after them, the date of the day.

And the words she wrote were these:

God, your love is so precious!
You protect people as a bird
    protects her young under
    her wings.
They eat the rich food in your
    house.
You let them drink from your
    river of pleasure.
You are the giver of life.
Your light lets us enjoy life.
                (Psalm 36:7-9)

A few days passed. The house was gloomy. But at last one evening there was rain all over the land, and when the farmer went out the next morning for his early walk by the cornfields, the corn had sprung up at last.

The young shoots burst out at once, and very soon all along the ridges were to be seen rows of tender blades, tinting the whole field with a delicate green. And day by day the farmer saw them, and was satisfied, but he spoke of other things and forgot to rejoice.

And when the farmer's wife asked him if the corn was doing well he answered, "Fairly well," and nothing more.

But his wife opened her Book, and wrote again on the very first page:

Who cuts a waterway for
the heavy rains?

*15*

And who sets a path for the
   thunderstorm to follow?
Who waters the land where no
   one lives?
Who waters the desert, that has
   no one in it?
Who sends the rain to satisfy
   the empty land,
   so grass begins to grow?     (Job 38:25-27)
No one understands how God
   spreads out the clouds.
No one understands how he
   thunders from where he
   lives.                              (Job 36:29)

The next few weeks were very peaceful. All nature seemed to rejoice in the fine weather. The corn-blades shot up strong and tall. They burst into flowers and gradually ripened into ears of grain. But the farmer still had some fault to find. He looked at the ears and saw that they were small. He grumbled and said:

"The yield will be less than it ought to be. The harvest will be bad."

Meanwhile a few weeks went by and a drought settled on the land. Rain was needed, so that the corn-ears might fill. Then one day the sky became full of heavy clouds, darkness spread over the land, a wild wind arose, and the roaring of thunder announced a storm. And such a storm! Along the ridges of corn-plants drove the rain-laden wind, and the plants bent down before it and rose again like the waves of the sea. They bowed down and they rose up. Only where the whirlwind was the strongest they fell to the ground and could not rise again.

And when the storm was over, the farmer saw here and there patches where the corn was pushed onto the ground, still dripping from the thundershower, and he grew angry, and forgot to think of the long ridges where the corn-plants were still standing tall and strong, and where the corn-ears were swelling with grain.

His face grew darker than ever. He was angry with the rain. He was angry with the sun because it did not shine. He blamed the corn because it might die before the harvest. But his wife wrote on the very first page of her Bible:

You water the mountains from
    above.
The earth is full of the things
    you made.
You make the grass for cattle
and vegetables for the use
    of man.
You make food grow from the
    earth.
You give us wine that makes
    happy hearts.
And you give us olive oil that
    makes our faces shine.
You give us bread that gives us
    strength. (Psalm 104:13-15)

Day by day the hours of sunshine were longer. Little by little the green corn-ears ripened into yellow, and the yellow turned into gold, and the abundant harvest was ready, and there were plenty of workers to help.

And the farmer's wife brought out her Bible and her husband read the words from God she had written starting with the day when the corn-seeds were held back by the first drought, and as he read a new heart seemed to grow within him, a heart that was thankful to the Lord of the Great Harvest. And he read aloud from the Book:

> You take care of the land and
>     water it,
> You make it very fertile.
> The rivers of God are full of
>     water:
> Grain grows because you make
>     it grow.
> You cause rain to fall on the
>     plowed fields.
> You soak them with water.
> You soften the ground with rain.
>     And then you bless it.
> You give the year a good harvest.
> You load the wagons with many
>     crops.

The desert is covered with grass.
The hills are covered with
    happiness.
The pastures are full of sheep.
The valleys are covered with
    grain.
Everything shouts and sings for
        joy.          (Psalm 65:9-13)

 **ope**

When we hope for something, we expect it to happen. But we know that sometimes we must wait for it with patience. We believe that God created us and the world, and that God plans good things for us. Sometimes frightening things happen, but we can place our hope in Jesus Christ and have faith that God's plan will always work in the end.

# JESUS AND THE FISHERMEN

*Luke 5:1-7, 11*

THERE were once some fishermen. Every night they went fishing. Every morning they sold the fish they had caught.

The fish were caught in big nets. Sometimes so many fish swam into the nets that holes were torn in them. After the fishermen had sold their fish they had to sit on the beach and tie up the holes in the nets. Tying up the holes took a long time.

One morning as the fishermen sat tying the holes in their nets a crowd of people gathered near them on the beach. Jesus was there. Jesus was telling stories. The people stood quietly. They listened to every word. The fishermen listened as they sat tying up the holes in the nets.

Jesus told the last story. The people began to move away. Jesus had been watching the fishermen sitting there tying the holes in their nets. At last there was no one on the beach except Jesus and the fishermen.

"Push the boat out into the deep water," said Jesus. "Let down the nets to catch fish."

Peter said, "All night we have been working. We let down the nets. We pulled them in. We caught no fish. But if you say to do it we shall let down the nets."

Slowly the nets dropped into the deep water. *Swish* came the sound of fishes swimming into the nets.

Slowly the fishermen began pulling in the nets. The nets were heavy. They were full of fish. The fishermen had to call another boat to help them.

When the two boats came to shore the fishermen had plenty of fish to sell. Jesus had helped the fishermen do their work.

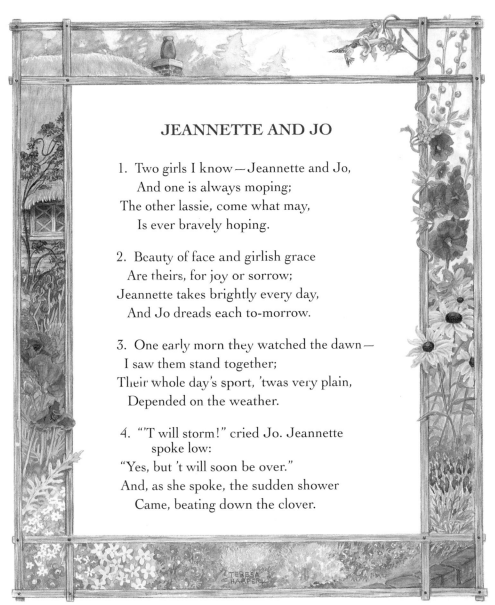

# JEANNETTE AND JO

1. Two girls I know—Jeannette and Jo,
   And one is always moping;
The other lassie, come what may,
   Is ever bravely hoping.

2. Beauty of face and girlish grace
   Are theirs, for joy or sorrow;
Jeannette takes brightly every day,
   And Jo dreads each to-morrow.

3. One early morn they watched the dawn—
   I saw them stand together;
Their whole day's sport, 'twas very plain,
   Depended on the weather.

4. "'T will storm!" cried Jo. Jeannette
      spoke low:
"Yes, but 't will soon be over."
And, as she spoke, the sudden shower
   Came, beating down the clover.

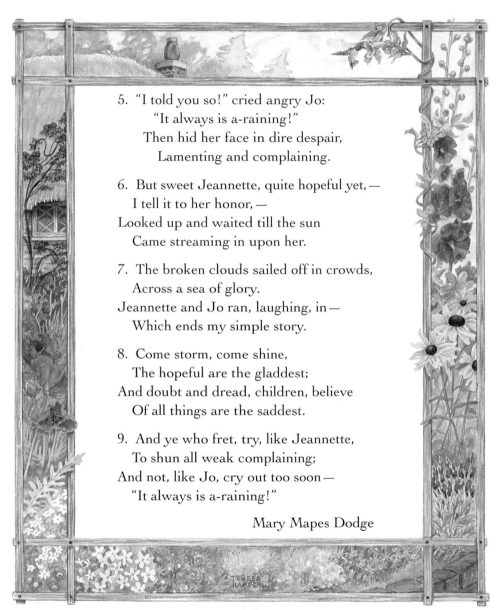

5. "I told you so!" cried angry Jo:
    "It always is a-raining!"
  Then hid her face in dire despair,
    Lamenting and complaining.

6. But sweet Jeannette, quite hopeful yet, —
    I tell it to her honor, —
  Looked up and waited till the sun
    Came streaming in upon her.

7. The broken clouds sailed off in crowds,
    Across a sea of glory.
  Jeannette and Jo ran, laughing, in —
    Which ends my simple story.

8. Come storm, come shine,
    The hopeful are the gladdest;
  And doubt and dread, children, believe
    Of all things are the saddest.

9. And ye who fret, try, like Jeannette,
    To shun all weak complaining;
  And not, like Jo, cry out too soon —
    "It always is a-raining!"

Mary Mapes Dodge

# Love

Love is a deep personal feeling for others. Christian love includes being loyal to others and taking responsibility for others. Jesus showed love clearly by his concern and care for others and by his life and death. We show our love for Jesus by taking care of other people.

TERESA
HARPER

# HOW FOUR FRIENDS HELPED

*Mark 2:1-4, 11-12; John 13:34; I John 3:18*

THERE was once a man who was sick. All day he lay on his bed. He could not walk.

Every day his friends came to see him. They had been to see Jesus. They told the sick man that Jesus helped sick people. Jesus helped people who were unhappy. Jesus talked about God. Jesus said, "Love one another."

The sick man lay on his bed. How wonderful it would be if he could see Jesus! But he could not walk. The sick man closed his eyes and lay still, wishing that he could go to see Jesus.

One day, the sick man lay on his bed. The door opened and four friends came in. "Jesus is only a little way down the road," said the four friends. "He is talking to the people in a house. There is a crowd at the door."

The sick man shook his head sadly. "I cannot walk," he said. "I cannot go."

The four friends whispered together. Then one friend took hold of one corner of his mattress. Another friend took another corner. There were four friends. There were four corners to the mattress. The sick man lay still on his mattress and the four friends carried him out of the door.

The sick man looked about. It had been a long time since he had been outdoors. He looked up and saw the blue sky. He felt the sunshine warm on his face. The sick man began to smile.

Down the road the four friends carried their sick friend. Soon they came to the house with the crowd of people standing near the door. Jesus was in that house.

But how could four men carry a man lying on his mattress through the crowd? The sick man did not smile now. Here he was so near Jesus, and he could not see him.

The four friends set the mattress down in the road. They stood thinking. They whispered together.

The house where Jesus was had a flat roof. It had steps up the outside to the roof. The four friends picked up the mattress. In a minute the sick man, lying on his mattress, was being carried up the steps to the roof.

The roof of the house had a place that could be opened to let in air and sunshine. The four friends set the mattress down on the roof. They opened the sliding window. They looked down into the house.

Yes, there Jesus was right below them. He was telling a story to the people who stood close about him.

The four friends tied ropes on the four corners of the mattress. Then each one holding a rope, they let down the sick man, lying on his mattress, until he was right at Jesus' feet. The crowd stepped back to make room for the sick man's mattress.

Jesus looked at the sick man. He saw that he could not move.

He was sorry for him. Jesus looked up. He saw the four friends looking down through the window in the roof.

Jesus smiled at the sick man. "Get up," he said. "Take your mattress and go home."

The sick man tried to get up. He stood on his feet. He took a step. He could walk. He picked up his mattress and walked out of the house. The four friends hurried down the outside stairs to go with him. The sick man was happy. The four friends were happy, too. They had helped.

# DAMON AND PYTHIAS

MORE than two thousand years ago two young men who were very close friends lived in Sicily. Their names were Damon and Pythias.

The ruler of the country, named Dionysius, was a cruel man. He put Pythias in prison and set a day for his death. Pythias had done nothing wrong but he had angered Dionysius.

The father and mother of Pythias lived far away. "May I go home to tell my father and mother good-by, and to arrange my affairs before I die?" asked Pythias.

The ruler laughed. "That is a strange request," he said. "Of course you would escape and you would never come back."

At that moment Damon stepped forward. "I am his friend," he said. "I will stay in prison until Pythias returns."

Then the ruler asked, "What will happen if Pythias does not return?"

"I will die for him," said Damon.

This surprised Dionysius very much. He put Damon in prison and Pythias went home. Weeks went by and Pythias did not return. At last the day of execution came, and Damon was led out to be put to death. He said, "Pythias will come if he is alive. I can trust him absolutely."

Just then soldiers ran up shouting: "Here he comes! Here comes Pythias!"

Yes, there was Pythias, breathless with hurrying. He had been shipwrecked on his journey and had been cast on shore many miles away.

Dionysius was greatly moved. "You are both free," he said. "I would give all I have for one such friend. Will you let me become a friend to you both?"

Ella Lymon Cabot

# LOVE YOUR ENEMIES

I SAY to you who are listening to me, love your enemies. Do good to those who hate you. Ask God to bless those who say bad things to you. Pray for those who are cruel to you. If anyone slaps you on your cheek, let him slap the other cheek too. If someone takes your coat, do not stop him from taking your shirt. Give to everyone who asks you. When a person takes something that is yours, don't ask for it back. Do for other people what you want them to do for you. If you love only those who love you, should you get some special praise for doing that? No! Even sinners love the people who love them! If you do good only to those who do good to you, should you get some special praise for doing that? No! Even sinners do that! If you lend things to people, always hoping to get something back, should you get some special praise for that? No! Even sinners lend to other sinners so that they can get back the same amount! So love your enemies. Do good to them, and lend to them without hoping to get anything back. If you do these things, you will have a great reward. . . . Yes, because God is kind even to people who are ungrateful and full of sin.

Luke 6:27-36

TERESA
HARPER

# oyalty

Christians show loyalty to others by staying by them no matter what. It is easy to be a friend when everything is going well, but true friends stick by each other through good times and bad times. Even if someone has hurt us, we can show God's love by continuing to love and to pray for that person. We can forgive them in our hearts and ask God to take care of them.

# RUTH HONORS NAOMI

*Ruth 1–4*

FAR AWAY in a land called Moab a poor widow started to return to her own home in the land of Israel. Ruth and Orpah, her two daughters-in-law, the wives of her sons who had just died, wished to go with her, for they could not think of the poor, old, sad mother returning all by herself on that long journey.

But after they had gone a little way, the old mother kissed them and said, "Go back to your home and native land!"

So Orpah kissed her good-by and returned, but Ruth clung to her mother-in-law and said: "Please do not ask me to leave you. I want to go anywhere you go and to live in whatever house you live in. I want your people in Israel to be my people and your God to be my God. I will stay with you forever."

Ruth knew that where Naomi was going she would be poor, and that they would have to work hard, but she loved her too much to leave her. Soon they saw the hills and then the houses of Bethlehem, Naomi's home. They settled down in that little town, but were so poor they did not know how to even get enough food to eat.

The time of the year had come when the farmers were beginning to cut the barley—the harvest time. It was the custom in that land to allow poor people to go into the fields and gather up the loose ears of barley that were left by the reapers; and Ruth went to glean a little food for herself and her mother. She happened to go into the field of a rich man named Boaz. By and by when Boaz came to see how the reapers were getting on, he saw Ruth working, and asked his reapers who she was. They told him that she was Naomi's daughter-in-law and how good she was being to Naomi.

Then Boaz called her to him and told her that she was welcome to glean in his field all through the harvest. He said: "I have heard all about your goodness to Naomi. God will reward you for your kindness."

At dinner time Boaz told her to sit down with the reapers, who gave her food and drink. She ate all she wished and still she had some left which in the evening she took home with her, with the barley she had gathered up, to Naomi.

At the end of the barley harvest, this great and good man, Boaz, fell in love with Ruth, and she became his wife. Naomi went to live with them in their large and beautiful house, and she always had all the things she needed. When a little son was born to Ruth, she named him Obed, and when he grew to be an old man, he was the grandfather of King David. So Ruth, the gleaner, who was kind and loyal to her mother-in-law, became the great-grandmother of the greatest King of Israel, and an ancestor of Jesus Christ, the King of Kings.

# THE SLAVE WHO BECAME A PRINCE

*Genesis 35:1-29; 37:12-36; 41-43*

JACOB had twelve sons, and Joseph was next to the youngest. He was the best loved of all, and his father showed how much he loved him by giving him a coat of many colors. This made his older brothers jealous and angry.

When Joseph was sixteen years old he dreamed that he was binding sheaves of grain in a field with his eleven brothers and his father and mother, and all the other sheaves bowed down to his sheaf. Another dream he had was that the sun and moon and eleven stars bowed down to him. When he told these dreams to his brothers, it made them even more angry. "What," they shouted, "do you think we will be bowing down to you?"

Soon after this the older brothers caught Joseph out in a field and put him down into a deep pit, and then sold him to camel drivers as a slave for twenty pieces of silver. Then they killed one of their own goats, dipped Joseph's coat of many colors into the blood, and taking it home, told their father that a wild animal had eaten Joseph. Jacob was very sad, and the brothers thought the dreamer would never tell any more of his dreams.

The camel-drivers sold Joseph as a slave in Egypt to a rich man who promoted him to be the chief ruler of his great house. It was a fine place for him. But one day someone told a very wicked lie about him, and he was cast into prison. But Joseph was so cheerful and kind and useful, even in prison, that he was soon placed over all the prisoners. When the king heard that Joseph had power to tell people the meaning of their dreams, he sent for him to tell the meaning of two dreams that were bothering him. Joseph explained the king's dreams to him. So Joseph was removed from prison to the king's palace, and was dressed in fine clothes, with a gold chain around his neck and a gold ring on his finger, and made ruler over all the land, next to the king.

Soon a great famine came to all the lands around Egypt. There was nothing to eat. But in Egypt, Joseph had filled big barns with grain. Joseph's ten brothers came from Canaan to Egypt to buy food to keep their families from starving. They were taken into the room where Joseph sat on a throne, and they bowed down before him. So the dreamer's dream came true, though they did not know it then. Joseph knew them, and treated them kindly without letting them know he was their brother. He longed to see his youngest brother, Benjamin, and told the others to bring him down with them when they came again, or they could have no more corn.

When they brought him, and Joseph looked into Benjamin's eyes, this great prince of Egypt burst into tears and said, "I am Joseph, your brother. You sold me as a slave, but God has taken care of me."

The brothers were afraid, but Joseph lovingly put his arms about their necks and kissed them. So they went home quickly and took their old father, Jacob, the good news. Then the brothers moved their families and their father to Egypt and Joseph took good care of them all.

## A SONG ABOUT GOD'S LOYALTY

I will always sing about the Lord's love.
I will tell of his loyalty from now on.
I will say, "Your love continues forever.
Your loyalty goes on and on like the sky."

Psalm 89:1-2

TERESA
HARPER+

TERESA
HARPER+

# Temperance

Temperance sounds like an old fashioned word, but it simply means taking care not to go overboard or to do too much of anything. We shouldn't eat or drink too much or the wrong things; we shouldn't worry too much; we shouldn't talk too loudly or too long; and we shouldn't put too much importance on money and the things it can buy.

# THE KING OF THE GOLDEN RIVER

ONCE there were three brothers, Hans, Swartz, and Gluck, the youngest. These three brothers owned a rich farm in a valley far up on the mountainside. The apples that grew there were so red, the corn so yellow, the grapes so blue, and everything was so fertile that it was called "Treasure Valley." On the very top of the mountain a river shone so bright and golden when lighted by the rays of the setting sun that people called it the "Golden River," but its waters flowed down on the other side of the mountain. The two older brothers were selfish and cruel. They beat their brother Gluck so cruelly one day for being kind to some one that the West Wind punished them by blowing, blowing, blowing so hard that everything became dry and the valley became a desert. Then the three brothers went to live in the town, and the two oldest went from bad to worse, until one day they said, "We have nothing left in the world but Gluck's golden pitcher." This pitcher was a gift from his uncle, which Gluck highly prized, but the cruel brothers ordered him, while they were away, to put it into the melting-pot and make it into gold spoons that they might secure money to support them. While the melting-pot with the gold pitcher in it was warming over the hot fire, Gluck looked out of the window and saw the sun reflecting its yellow glow in the Golden River, far up on the mountain crest. He sighed, "How fine it would be if only that river were really gold. We wouldn't be poor then!" "It wouldn't be fine at all," said a thin little voice from the melting-pot. "Pour me out! Pour me out! I'm too hot," continued the thin little

*44*

voice. It was the King of the Golden River, who peeped out of the melting-pot and said: "Whoever climbs to the top of the mountain where the Golden River begins, and pours in three drops of water, shall find the river turned into gold. But whoever fails at the first trial can have no other, and will be changed into a big boulder." With these words the King of the Golden River vanished up the chimney. Just then the two brothers came in, and when they saw the golden pitcher all melted away and vanished in smoke up the chimney, they beat poor Gluck black and blue for his carelessness. When Gluck told them what the King of the Golden River had said, at first they would not believe him, and then they quarreled so terribly

over which should be the first to go, that a policeman came and Swartz was thrown into prison. Then Hans said, "I will be the first to get the gold." He took a bottle of water and climbed up, up, up the mountainside until he met a dog so thirsty that his tongue hung from his mouth. Hans gave the dog a kick and passed on until he met a little child, who said, "I'm so thirsty." But Hans gave the child a slap and passed on until he met a little old man, who cried, "Water! Water! I'm dying for water!" Hans spoke bad words and passed on, drinking up all the water himself. So when he came to the source of the Golden River he found that all his water was gone, and he did not have even three drops to put into the river. Then, in a rage, he threw the empty bottle into the stream, and immediately there was great thunder and lightning, and Hans was changed into a big boulder.

When Hans did not return, Gluck went to work in a goldsmith's shop to earn money enough to get Swartz out of prison. As soon as he was released he said, "Now I will try to get the gold." So Swartz took a bottle of water and climbed up, up, up the mountainside, passing the poor, thirsty dog, the little child, and the little old man dying of thirst, without so much as sharing one drop of water with them. When he came to the source of the Golden River he found that all his water was gone and he did not have even three drops to pour into the river. Then, in a rage, he threw the empty bottle into the stream, and immediately there was great thunder and lightning, and Swartz was changed into a big boulder beside his brother.

Gluck waited long for his brothers to return, but when they did not come he took a bottle of water and started to climb up, up, up the mountainside until he came to the poor thirsty dog, and the little child, and then the little old man, with each of whom Gluck kindly shared the water from his bottle, and when he reached the top of the mountain he found he had plenty of water still in his bottle. So he poured in three drops of his water into the heart of the river, but, to his surprise, he found that the river did not change into gold. The water began to flow down the other side of the mountain toward Treasure Valley. He was disappointed and sad. Then the King of the Golden River appeared again and said, "Follow the stream!" Then he noticed, as he went down the mountainside, that everywhere the river flowed flowers and vines and fruit trees blossomed, and soon all

Treasure Valley was one rich, beautiful garden again. Then he saw that the river was indeed, as the King had said, a River of Gold. After that Gluck lived in a beautiful home in Treasure Valley. His apples were red, his corn was yellow, his grapes were blue, and everything became prosperous again. But the hungry and thirsty were never once sent empty away.

*—Adapted from John Ruskin*

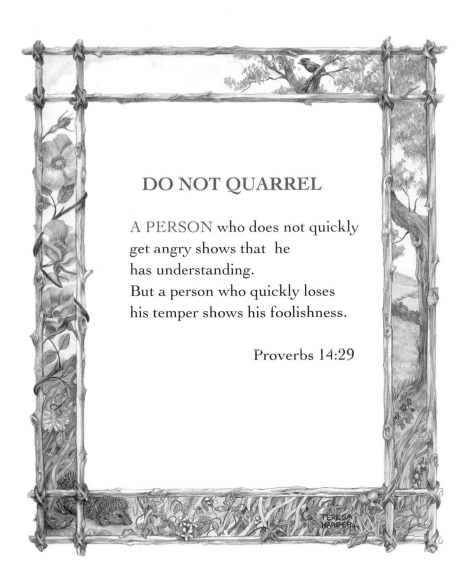

# DO NOT QUARREL

A PERSON who does not quickly
get angry shows that  he
has understanding.
But a person who quickly loses
his temper shows his foolishness.

Proverbs 14:29

# FOUR BOYS WHO KEPT STRONG

*Daniel 1*

FOUR BOYS, who were great friends, were taken from their homes and carried far away into a great city in a foreign land to live among strangers. One day the King ordered his officers to select from among the Jewish captive boys four of the brightest, and these four boys were chosen and brought into the King's palace to be educated for royal service.

Thinking it a great honor to them, and that it would make them strong, the King ordered that these boys should by given a daily supply of the rich food and wine that he and all his

household, including his soldiers, received. But the very first time the silver tray, with all of those dainties, was brought to the four friends, one of them, whose name was Daniel, said to the officer who took charge of them,

"Please take this food away and bring us fresh vegetables to eat and water to drink."

The officer laughed and said, "I am afraid that if you do not eat this rich food you will look thin and not as strong as the other students. The King will be so angry with me that he will cut off my head!"

But Daniel said, "Let us try the plain food for ten days. Then

compare us to the other boys who eat the King's rich food and drink his wine, and see."

The officer agreed. At the end of the time, Daniel and his friends were stronger than all the other boys. They were allowed to eat their way for the entire three years of their training.

At the end of that time, all the students were called before the King, who sat on a golden throne. The King saw that these four were stronger than all the rest and that they knew more than the magicians and astrologers in all his kingdom. So, Daniel, Shadrach, Meshach, and Abednego, these four friends who were true to their principles, showed after all that they kept their health and were stronger and better by going without the rich food and royal wine.

 ourage

To have courage means to be strong and to stand up for what we believe is right. We often have to be strong about small things like being kind to someone others treat unkindly. Sometimes we have to show courage by choosing not to do something, like taking drugs, when all our friends are doing it.

# THE LIONS' DEN

*Daniel 6:1-23*

DANIEL did very good work for the king of Babylon, better than anyone else. So the king decided to put Daniel in charge of the whole kingdom. That made many important people very angry. They wanted to get rid of Daniel. They tried to catch Daniel doing something wrong, but they could not.

These people saw Daniel pray to God three times a day. That gave them an idea. Daniel's enemies got the king to make this law: "For the next thirty days, any person who prays to any god or man except the king will be thrown into a pit filled with lions."

Daniel knew the law, but Daniel still prayed to God three times a day.

When Daniel's enemies saw him praying to God, they went to the king and said, "Your Majesty, you signed an order that for the next thirty days, anyone who prays to any god or man except you will be thrown into a pit filled with lions."

The king replied, "Yes, that is a strict order, a law which cannot be changed."

Then they said to the king, "Daniel, one of the exiles from Judah, does not respect Your Majesty or obey the law. He prays to his god three times a day."

When the king heard this, he was very upset. He did his best to rescue Daniel, but he could not. At sunset, Daniel was thrown into a pit filled with lions. The king said to Daniel, "May the god, whom you serve so loyally, rescue you."

All night long the king could not sleep. At dawn he got up and hurried to the pit. When he got there, he called out anxiously, "Daniel, servant of the living God! Was the god you serve so loyally able to save you from the lions?"

Daniel answered, "God sent his angel to shut the mouths of the lions so that they would not hurt me. He did this because he knew that I was innocent and because I have not wronged you, Your Majesty."

The king was overjoyed and gave orders for Daniel to be pulled out of the pit.

# POCAHONTAS

POCAHONTAS was a beautiful Native American girl, the daughter of the great chief, Powhatan. She was so good and kind that she was loved by all the tribe over which her father ruled.

Although Pocahontas was a Native American princess, she learned to cook and to sew and to weave mats, just like the other girls. She spent many happy hours decorating her dresses with pretty colored shells and beads.

One day, when she was twelve years old, one of Powhatan's scouts came to him and told him a white man had been captured and brought to the village.

"He is a wonderful man," said the scout. "He can talk to his friends by making marks on paper, and he can make a fire without flint."

"Bring him here," said the chief, and Captain John Smith was brought before Powhatan.

The chief received the prisoner, and talked with him, asking him many questions.

Captain Smith told the Native Americans that the earth was round, and that the sun chased the night around it. He said that the sun that set in the west at night was the same sun that rose in the east in the morning. He showed them his compass and told them how it guided him through the forest.

At last the Native Americans began to fear him, thinking that so wise and powerful a man might do them some harm. So, after holding him as a prisoner for many days, they decided to put him to death.

In the meantime Captain Smith and Pocahontas had become the best of friends. He told her many stories of his childhood in a land across the sea, of the children who lived there, of their toys and games, their homes and schools, and how they learned to read and write.

So when Pocahontas learned that her dear friend must die, she felt very sad, and tried to think of some way of saving his life.

And she did save his life, for just as Captain Smith was to be killed, the child threw her arms around his neck, and begged her father to spare the white man's life, for her sake.

Powhatan loved his little daughter, and wished to please her in everything, so he promised to set the prisoner free, and to send him at once to his friends.

Pocahontas often visited Captain Smith, and learned to know and love his friends. In later years she went to England to see all the things he had told her about during his captivity.

# THE WORD OF GOD

My lips will tell about
    all the laws you have spoken.
I enjoy living by your rules
    as people enjoy great riches.
I think about your orders
    and study your ways.
I enjoy obeying your demands.
      And I will not forget your word.

Psalm 119:13-16

 # rudence

Prudence is thinking ahead and planning to do the right or the best thing in any happening. If we listen for God's voice before we act, we will be able to make the right decision.

# THE BABY IN A BASKET-BOAT

*Exodus 1; 2: 1-10*

LONG, LONG AGO, a little boy was born in a Hebrew home, at a time when a cruel king of Egypt ordered all Hebrew boy babies to be thrown into the river Nile. But his mother was determined to keep him safe. She hid him in the house and prayed for God to keep him safe. She hid him carefully for three months. Then, being afraid someone might hear him, she went to the river and gathered some long, strong grasses that grew there and braided them together, making a small basket and shaping it like a boat. To make it warm and dry inside, and to keep it from sinking under the water, she painted it with tar inside and out.

Early one morning, when all was ready, the mother took her baby boy quietly sleeping in the basket-boat, and went down to the river Nile. The baby's sister, Miriam, followed close behind them. The mother hid the basket among the tall grasses near the shore, and prayed to God to keep her baby safe. Miriam was left hiding in the tall grass near-by to see what would happen to her little brother in his new bed.

Very soon a princess, the daughter of the cruel king of Egypt, with her maids, came down to the river to bathe. Quickly she spied the basket-boat and cried, "What is that floating on the water among the tall grasses? Bring it to me."

One of the maids ran and picked up the basket and brought it to the princess. When she opened it, there was a beautiful baby

boy! The child was wide awake, and seeing the strange face, began to cry. "It is one of the Hebrew babies," she said. "I have found him, and I will keep him as my own little baby boy. I will name him Moses."

Miriam was watching from her hiding place in the tall grasses. She ran out and said, "Shall I bring a nurse for the baby?"

"Yes," said the princess.

Miriam ran home as fast as she could and whom do you suppose she brought? The baby's own mother! And the princess told her to take him home and care for him, for she loved him as her very own, and the king would not harm him.

So the prayer that Moses' mother made to God to take care of her little baby boy in the basket-boat was answered. And Moses grew up to be a great and good man.

# PLANTING AN ORCHARD

ONCE there was a man who wanted to plant an orchard of apple trees. He sent to a nursery for some young plants, and when they came all wrapped up in a good bundle, he thought of what fine trees he was going to have, and the beautiful apples they would bear.

The bundle came just about the time the man was starting to town on some business. So he sent off at once for a man who knew how to plant trees, and said to him, "Here are my young apple trees, and I want you to plant them for me. I shall be gone all day," and he showed the man where to plant them.

When he came back later in the afternoon the man had planted only six trees. The owner was surprised and said, "It seems to me you work very slowly."

The man replied, "Yes, but I do my work thoroughly. You see I dug great holes so that the roots of the young trees might not be broken or cramped; then I hauled rich earth from the woods, and mixed it well with the top soil; then I packed the earth carefully around the roots so that it would be firm; and then I watered each plant until it was thoroughly soaked. All that takes time, and one must not be in a hurry about planting a tree if he expects it to live and flourish."

"That sounds very fine," said the owner, "but it is too slow a way for me. I could have planted five times as many in a day. You take too much trouble." So he dismissed the man and the next day he planted his orchard in his own way.

He dug the holes just large enough to hold the roots by

twisting them together, and many of the rootlets were broken or injured as they were forced into place; he did not get the soft rich earth from the woods, nor was he careful in packing the dirt around the roots, and then he did not fill the holes with water.

"Now, see there," he said to himself, "I have planted a whole orchard in one day."

But see what happened! The trees the owner planted so carelessly lived for a while, and put out a few leaves. They bore some little apples, and then the owner cut them down. But the six trees the other man planted grew up strong and healthy. In a few years they were well shaped and tall and began to bear quantities of beautiful apples. When the owner was an old man they still were standing, and everybody would say, "What wonderful apple trees! What splendid fruit!"

But the old man knew he could have had a whole orchard like that if he had planted them all as the six were planted.

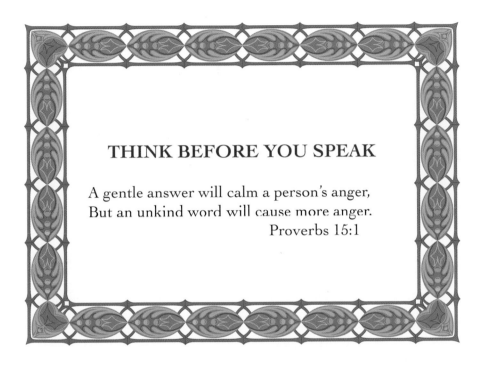

## THINK BEFORE YOU SPEAK

A gentle answer will calm a person's anger,
But an unkind word will cause more anger.

Proverbs 15:1

TERESA
HARPER

# Humility

Humility is not thinking of ourselves as better than others. We often say that Jesus showed humility when he left heaven and came to earth to live just as we do. We try to live like Jesus by putting others first.

# THE KING WITH THE BASIN AND THE TOWEL

*John 13:1-17*

ONE evening Jesus and his friends were gathered together at supper in an upper room of a house which had been loaned for this special meal. Jesus and his friends had walked a long distance that day over a rough and dusty road and their feet, in the loose sandals, were sore and dusty. Near the door stood a pitcher filled with cool, fresh water, and also a basin and a towel, but there was no servant at the door to wash their feet when they removed their sandals and passed to their places around the table.

Each of the twelve friends of Jesus was thinking about which one of them would get the best seat in Jesus' kingdom, and each wanted to have the highest place of honor at the table. No one had offered to take the basin and the towel, but rather they were even quarreling over which should recline next to Jesus at the head of the table.

Jesus didn't say a word. He arose from the table, went quietly over to the water-jar, laid aside his outer cloak, and tied a towel around his waist, like a servant. Then he took up the basin, filled it with water, and began to wash his friends' feet, one after the other, and to wipe them with the towel.

Jesus was the King of heaven and earth as well as their friend. One of them should have offered to do this. But no one thought of serving the others but Jesus. So, when he had finished washing the feet of all of them, he put on his outer cloak again, took his place at the table, and said, "The person who wants to be the greatest of all must first become the servant of all."

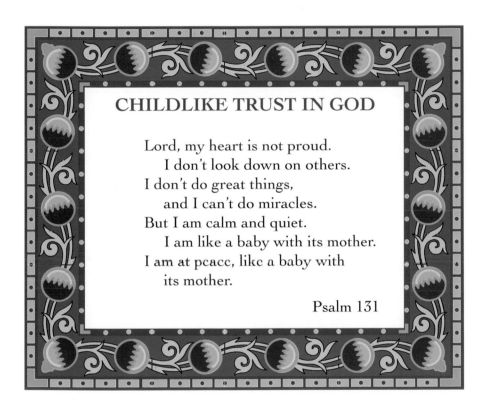

### CHILDLIKE TRUST IN GOD

Lord, my heart is not proud.
    I don't look down on others.
I don't do great things,
    and I can't do miracles.
But I am calm and quiet.
    I am like a baby with its mother.
I am at peace, like a baby with
    its mother.

Psalm 131

# THE LITTLE PINE TREE WHO WISHED FOR NEW LEAVES

A LITTLE pine tree grew in the forest. It was not happy because it did not have leaves like the maple, oaks, and other trees that grew near.

"Why must I have only green needles on my branches?" it sighed. "How I wish that I might have leaves of shining gold and be different from all the other trees in the forest."

Now, the angel of the forest heard the little pine tree, and that night while it slept, its wish came true. The next morning the little pine tree had leaves of shining gold, and was very happy.

"How beautiful I am!" it thought. "What must the other trees think of me now!"

How foolish was the little pine tree! In the night a man came to the woods. He picked every one of the gold leaves and put them in a box.

"What shall I do?" cried the little tree. "I see now that it will not do to have leaves of gold. If I could only have leaves of glass, I would be happy again."

The angel of the forest, who was listening, again granted the little tree's wish, and the next morning when it awoke its branches were covered with leaves of clear, shining glass. Again the little tree was happy, but not for long. After a while the sunbeams hid and clouds gathered in the sky. Lower and lower they hung, and by and by the rain came. How the wind did blow! The glass leaves shook in the wind, and struck against the branches and against one another. Soon the leaves were shattered, and little bits of glass covered the ground. Not a leaf was left on the branches!

"Ah, me!" sighed the little tree again. "Perhaps I should not wish to be better than the other trees. If I could only have green leaves like theirs, I would be happy."

A third time the angel of the forest granted the little tree's wish. When morning came it was covered with big shiny green leaves. By and by a goat came along and ate every one of the nice juicy leaves for his dinner.

"Dear me!" said the little tree. "Perhaps it is best after all that I have only my green needles! If I could only have them back!"

While it slept that night the angel of the forest touched it and the next morning it awoke to find long green needles covering its branches. "I like the needles better than the gold, or the glass, or the green leaves," said the pine tree. The little pine never complained again. The birds were happy, too, for in the winter it was the little pine tree that kept them safe and warm.

# rustworthiness

People who are trustworthy are honest and truthful. We can believe in them. We can trust them just as we trust God. God expects us to be honest and truthful with others.

# SCATTERED SEEDS

RITA was feeling very unhappy. She hadn't been really happy for two whole days—not since she had repeated a story about her friend Marie that she wasn't sure was true.

She knew she would never feel comfortable about it until she had talked it over with Mother, but she hated to have her know. Finally, she couldn't stand it any longer, and throwing her arms around her mother's neck, she told her all about it.

Mother looked very sorry, but all she said was, "Rita, I want you to go to the big field down by the hardware store and gather a handful of the brown milkweed pods. On your way home, open the pods and let the little winged seeds fly away. Then come back to me."

This sounded like a very easy punishment, and Rita quickly found some milkweed plants. She ran and hopped and jumped through the field, tossing from her hands the silky, floating seeds. Pink-cheeked and smiling, she came back to her mother.

"Now," said her mother, "go back to the field, and, on the way, gather the seeds you have scattered, every one, and bring them to me."

The little girl tried to do as her mother asked, but she found that the wind had scattered the delicate seeds far and wide. They were stuck in the leaves of the trees that grew along the street, they nestled in the earth under the hedges, and they floated gently in the little river that ran through the town.

Some of them had found a new field, where they settled themselves to establish new colonies of milkweed plants.

At last, discouraged and almost in tears, Rita went

back to her mother with only a few of the seeds she had
scattered.

"My little daughter," Mother said, "this is what happened
when you scattered unkind words about Marie, whether they

were false or true. Unkind words are like little sparks of fire falling in dried grass; they may cause great damage—at home, perhaps, or at school, or even in the world. And words once spoken are scattered like milkweed seeds."

# THE NECKLACE OF TRUTH

ONCE there was a little girl named Coralie. She had only one fault. She told lies. Her parents tried to cure her in many ways but nothing they did worked. Finally they decided to take her to see a wise man named Merlin.

Now Merlin lived in a glass palace. He loved truth. It is said that he could smell when someone was a teller of lies, and that the odor made him sick. Sure enough, when Coralie came into the room, he had to hold his handkerchief in front of his face!

Coralie's mother began to explain the reason for their coming. But Merlin stopped her.

"I know all about your daughter, my good lady," he said. "She is one of the greatest liars in the world. She makes me sick."

Merlin's face looked so stern that Coralie hid her face under her mother's cloak. Her father stood before her to keep her from harm.

"Don't be afraid," said Merlin. "I am not going to hurt your little girl. I only wish to give her a present."

He opened a drawer and took from it a magnificent amethyst necklace. It was fastened with a shining clasp of diamonds.

Merlin put the necklace on Coralie's neck and said, "Go in peace, my friends. Your little daughter carries with her a sure guardian of the truth."

Then he looked sternly at Coralie and said, "In a year I shall come for my necklace. Do not dare to take it off for a single moment. If you do, harm will come to you."

"Oh, I shall always love to wear it! It is so beautiful!" cried

Coralie. And this is the way she came by the wonderful Necklace of Truth.

The day after Coralie returned home she was sent to school. The little girls crowded around her. There was a cry of admiration at the sight of the necklace.

"Where did you get it?" they asked.

"I was sick for a long time," Coralie replied. "When I got well, Mamma and Papa gave me the necklace."

A loud cry rose from all the children all at once. The diamonds of the clasp had grown dim. They now looked like coarse glass.

"Yes, indeed, I have been sick. What are you making such a fuss about?"

At this second falsehood the amethysts changed to ugly yellow stones. A new cry arose. Coralie was frightened at the strange behavior of her necklace.

"I have been to see the wise man, Merlin," she said very humbly.

Immediately the necklace looked as beautiful as before. But the children teased her.

"You shouldn't laugh," said Coralie, "for Merlin was very glad to see us. He sent his carriage to meet us. Merlin's palace is all of gold. He met us at the door and led us to the dining room. There stood a long table covered with delicious things to eat. First of all we ate — "

Coralie stopped, for the children were laughing till the tears rolled down their cheeks. She glanced at the necklace and shuddered. With each new falsehood, the necklace had become longer and longer, till it already dragged on the ground.

"Coralie, you are stretching the truth," cried the little girls.

"Well, I confess it. We walked, and we stayed there only five minutes."

The necklace shrank at once to its proper size.

"The necklace — the necklace — where did it come from?"

"He gave it to me without saying a word. I think —"

She did not have time to finish. The necklace grew shorter and shorter till it choked her. She gasped for breath.

"You are keeping back part of the truth," cried her schoolmates.

"He said — that I was — one of the biggest — liars in the world."
The necklace loosened, but Coralie still cried with pain.

"That was why Merlin gave me the necklace. He said that it would make me truthful. What a fool I have been to be proud of it!"

Her playmates were sorry for her. "If I were in your place," said one of them, "I should send back the necklace. Why don't you take it off?"

Poor Coralie did not wish to speak, but the stones of the necklace began to dance up and down and to make a terrible clatter.

"There is something you have not told us," laughed the little girls.

"I like to wear it."

Oh, how the diamonds and amethysts danced! It was worse than ever.

"Tell us what you are keeping back."

"Well, I see I can hide nothing. Merlin told me not to take it off. He said great harm would come to me if I disobeyed."

Thanks to the Necklace of Truth, Coralie became a truthful child. Long before the year had passed, Merlin came for his necklace. He needed it for another child who told falsehoods.

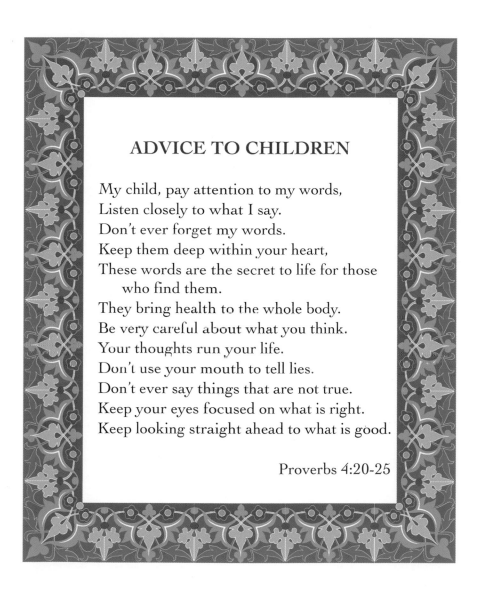

# ADVICE TO CHILDREN

My child, pay attention to my words,
Listen closely to what I say.
Don't ever forget my words.
Keep them deep within your heart,
These words are the secret to life for those
    who find them.
They bring health to the whole body.
Be very careful about what you think.
Your thoughts run your life.
Don't use your mouth to tell lies.
Don't ever say things that are not true.
Keep your eyes focused on what is right.
Keep looking straight ahead to what is good.

Proverbs 4:20-25

# Responsibility

God expects us to take good care of the earth and of all God's creation. Sometimes this means working. Our work may be very simple or it may be very hard, but God always expects us to do our very best. Sometimes responsibility means choosing to do the right thing, by sticking with our work or our friends when it would be easier to quit.

# WHEN EVERYONE HELPED

*Nehemiah 2:17-18b; 3:1-32; 4:6; 6:15*

REUBEN woke up early. He could hear the *pound, pound, pound* of the hammers. He jumped up from his mat in a hurry and dressed. He knew that the workmen would be depending on him again today.

For many days now, Reuben had been watching the men build the walls around the city. He had heard Nehemiah tell the people that the broken walls and gates should be mended to make their city beautiful.

"I have found wood and stone with which to repair the wall," Nehemiah said. "If everyone builds a part of the wall, we will soon have it finished."

Reuben's father was one of the workmen. He worked hard for a few hours and then would come home to rest before starting in again. One day Reuben's father said: "Many of the boys are taking water to the workmen. You are big enough now to help, too."

"I will help, Father," said Reuben. "Some of the men are working near our house. I will give them water to drink."

So every morning when Reuben heard the *pound, pound, pound* of the hammers he knew that it was time to get the water skin ready.

Reuben liked to watch the men lay one brick on top of another. Higher and higher went the wall. It was so high now that the workmen had to use a ladder to reach the top. One day

Reuben's father let him climb the ladder and look over the wall. He could look all over the city. He could see the other boys taking water to the workmen.

One morning when Reuben was standing by his water skin, one of the workmen came down the ladder.

"Are you thirsty?" asked Reuben.

"Oh, yes," answered the workman. "The sun is hot and it will help to have a cool drink."

Reuben filled the shiny cup with water and handed it to the workman.

"I do not know how we could do our work without your help," the workman said.

"My mother helps, too," said Reuben. "She cooks food for the men and takes it to them while they are at work."

"It is like Nehemiah said," replied the workman, "with everyone helping, mothers and fathers and boys and girls, the wall will soon be finished."

Day after day the hammers went *pound, pound, pound.* Day after day Reuben stood by the water skin to pour out cool, fresh water for the thirsty workers.

Soon the wall was finished. The gates were in place. The city looked beautiful again. How glad the fathers and mothers and children were that they could help!

# THE KING'S PAGE

THERE was once a little boy who wished very, very much to be a page in the palace of the King. He lived in a tiny house at the foot of a hill and at the tip-top of the hill stood the palace, shining bright in the sun with many sparkling towers and minarets. Once a day the great gates of the castle grounds opened wide and out came the King and all his retinue, riding down the hill and past the little boy's house and on to the woods to hunt.

Oh, but the sight was wonderful! White, and brown, and black horses pranced by, their trappings as bright as gold. The King rode ahead, dressed in his bright hunting costume and followed by all his retainers. There were the little page boys,too, manly and straight, as they walked at the end of the procession in their green velvet doublets and wearing feathers in their caps.

"I want to be a page. I want to be a page. I want to walk behind the King," said the little boy every day when the King went by.

And one day came his chance.

"Come with me," said a messenger who waited at the doorway of the little boy's house. "You are needed at the castle."

So the little boy kissed his mother good-bye and climbed up the hill with the messenger. He was quite happy and all the way his joyful heart beat time to the tramp, tramp, tramp of his stout leather shoes. And his heart sang, too.

"I shall see the King's gold throne. I shall eat my supper from a bowl of silver. I shall wear a green velvet cloak and have a feather in my hat," he thought.

But when they came to the top of the hill the little boy felt, as he looked down, that he was a long way from home. He was surprised, too, to see how dark and gloomy the old castle looked. Instead of going straight to the throne room, he was taken through long stone passages to the kitchen, a great, busy room. Here the messenger left him.

"Where is my sword?" the little boy asked, and the King's cook, laughing, put a wooden ladle in his hand with which he was to stir the soup in the broth pot.

"I want to sit at the foot of the King's throne," begged the little boy; but one of the maids showed him a rough wooden bench with no back where he was to sit and polish the copper pots after the soup was finished.

"Where is my green velvet cloak?" he questioned at last, and at that all the scullery boys in the kitchen laughed and they tied a big, coarse apron on him. "This is your new uniform," they said.

The little boy was not used to crying when things went wrong, so he began to work as hard as he could in the King's kitchen. It was not so bad a place, after all, and always warm and cheerful with the odors of basting fowl, savory sauces and spiced puddings. Every one had something to do every minute of the time and whether it was sweeping or cutting up vegetables, everybody did it very well.

"This is a huge household to feed," said the King's cook, "and it is quite as important to pare a potato neatly as to wield a sword."

The little boy listened and decided to learn how to be a good little kitchen helper. So he searched the woods and fields for the rare herbs that helped to make the King's broth tasty, and he stirred the broth so hard that it was more perfectly blended than ever before. He sat on his hard wooden bench and polished the copper pots until they caught the sunshine. And he sang at his work like a little brown thrush, all day long. And so, in working, he forgot to wish for a sword, a green velvet cloak and a feather.

After the little boy had been a helper in the King's kitchen for many months, the big door opened one morning. There stood the same messenger who had called for him at his house.

"The King wishes to see the page who sings at his work," said the messenger. "Come." He reached out his hand to the little boy.

"But I am not a page yet, I have not learned to be a page," he said.

"You have been learning here in the kitchen,"—the messenger beckoned to the little boy to follow him. "A boy who can serve a cook can serve a King."

So the little boy was a page and carried a sword and wore a green velvet cloak and had a feather in his cap. And he walked behind the King in the procession.

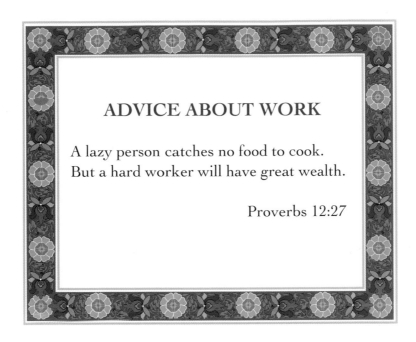

## ADVICE ABOUT WORK

A lazy person catches no food to cook.
But a hard worker will have great wealth.

Proverbs 12:27